WORLD*focus*
Senegal
ALISON BROWNLIE

Contents

Note to the reader
In this book some words in the text are printed in **bold** type. This shows that the word is listed in the glossary on page 30. The glossary gives a brief explanation of words that may be new to you.

Introduction

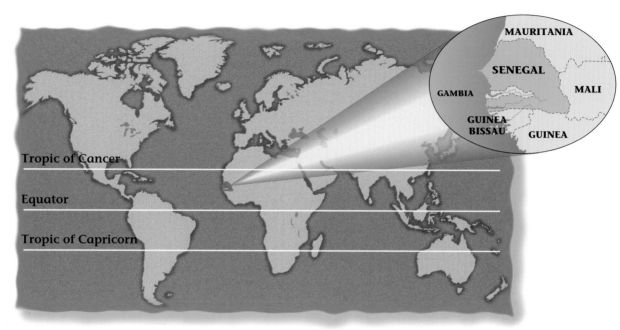

Tropic of Cancer

Equator

Tropic of Capricorn

MAURITANIA

SENEGAL

GAMBIA

MALI

GUINEA BISSAU

GUINEA

You may not have heard very much about Senegal. It's not often mentioned on the news. That doesn't mean that nothing happens there, or that it isn't an interesting country. In this book you will learn something about Senegal, its rich culture, and its people.

△ **Where is Senegal?**

About the Country

Senegal is the most westerly country on the continent of Africa. If you stand on the shore and look out across the Atlantic Ocean, there is nothing between you and the Americas. From here you can see beautiful sunsets over the sea. People have called Senegal "the Land of the Setting Sun."

Look at the map above. You can see that another country, Gambia, lies within Senegal. It follows the Gambia River and slots into Senegal like a sleeve. It is almost an **enclave.** Southwest Senegal is therefore separated from the rest of the country.

Senegal is one of the smaller countries in Africa. It is just a little smaller than the state of Nebraska in the United States. It has a population of $8\frac{1}{2}$ million. It is a very flat country.

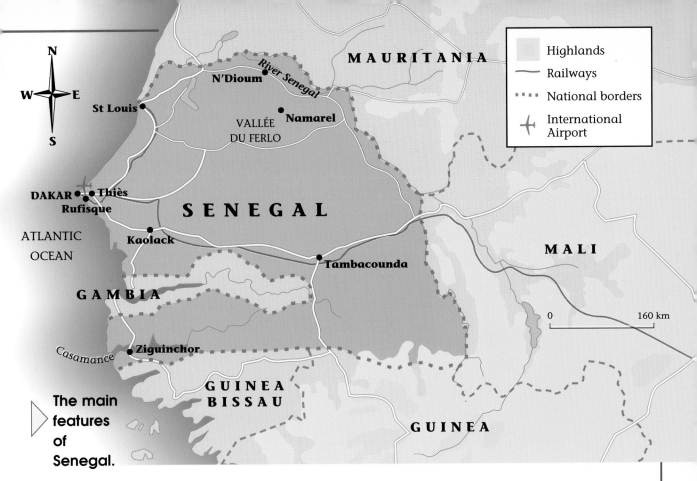

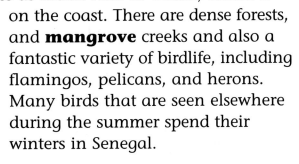

> The main features of Senegal.

> One of Senegal's beautiful beaches on the Atlantic coast.

Forests and Deserts

Senegal has a **tropical** climate, but it varies quite a lot. In the southwest it is hot and wet. On the edge of the **monsoon** area, it has four to five months of rain. This is almost three times as much rain as Dakar, which is on the coast. There are dense forests, and **mangrove** creeks and also a fantastic variety of birdlife, including flamingos, pelicans, and herons. Many birds that are seen elsewhere during the summer spend their winters in Senegal.

The north is also hot, but this area is part of the **Sahel,** on the edge of the Sahara desert, and is very dry. Rain falls only between July and October. And even then, people don't know exactly when, or if, it will rain. The soil is sandy, and the hot **harmattan** winds cause sandstorms that last for days.

3

The People

People have lived in the area now called Senegal for many thousands of years.

Recent History

In 1450, Europeans visited Senegal looking for gold and precious metals. Then, 100 years later, more Europeans came to take people to the Caribbean to work on plantations to produce cotton and sugar for people in Europe. All over West Africa, men, women, and children were captured and sent in ships over the Atlantic Ocean in appalling conditions. Millions of Africans died on the way.

Today, many African Americans in the United States and the Caribbean are descended from these slaves. Some visit Senegal to see where their ancestors came from. They usually visit the Isle of Gorée.

Senegal was a colony of France from the middle of the 19th century until 1960, when it became independent. The French considered it as part of France, and people born in certain towns were full French citizens.

▽ **Slave house on Gorée, which was a collecting station for slaves**

People and Language

The people of Senegal belong to many different groups—the Wolof, Peulh, Serer, Toucouleur, Mandinga, and Diola. Two million people belong to the largest ethnic group, the Wolof. There are six national languages, but 80 percent of the people speak Wolof. Children in schools are taught in French, which is the official language, but it is unusual to hear people speak it outside the main towns.

Politics and Religion

Most people in Senegal are **Muslims.** The Muslim leaders, called marabouts, are a very powerful group in Senegal.

Senegal is a **multiparty democracy** and has a good **human-rights** reputation, although the government has not always lived up to this. Newspapers in Senegal are allowed to say what they want, and there are active trade unions. These are all signs that the government believes its people should have freedom of expression.

△ Senegal's daily newspaper is called "Le Soleil," which is French for "The Sun."

Culture

In Senegal there is a rich **oral tradition** in which stories and histories are told by **griots.** People say that when a griot dies it is like a library burning down because of all the stories that are lost. The stringed kora and talking drum are popular instruments, and music is played at every opportunity. Senegal has several world-famous musicians, including Youssou N'dour and Baba Maal.

Where Do People Live?

△ Dakar, with the Isle of Gorée in the background

In Senegal more people live in towns than they do in most other African countries. Almost half the population live in Dakar, the capital, and towns such as Thiès, Ziguinchor, Kaolack, and St. Louis.

Living in the Country

Most people living in country villages grow food or keep animals. In areas where there is more rain and the land is fertile, there are more villages. In the north, where it rains less, the people are **nomadic** for part of the year. Most villages have a school and a health center, but a few do not. Some children cannot go to school, because the schools are too far away.

Sometimes after a bad **drought** crops may die, so there is little food to eat. People leave their villages to look for work in the cities or towns, or even abroad. It is often men who go, sending money back to the women who look after the families. If they can, people living in the city go back to their villages to help with cattle or the crops at busy times.

Living in the City

Dakar, the capital city, is built on a **peninsula** and is cooled by sea breezes. It has high-rise office buildings, hotels, restaurants, elegant shops, and traffic jams. Some people think Dakar is a lot like Paris. You can even buy French bread for breakfast! It is also an important seaport, **exporting** peanuts and fish products and importing manufactured goods that the country needs.

△ A delivery of baguettes to a village

Dakar is growing very quickly, as people leave the countryside and move to the city. Many of them live in areas of poor housing on the outskirts of the city, known as "bidonvilles" or shanty towns. There are few jobs, and many people are unemployed. People find whatever work they can. Many women have set up small businesses, such as hair braiding, doughnut making, and selling fruit in the market. There are many beggars asking for money. In Muslim culture, giving to the poor is very important, and people give money readily.

▽ Shops in Dakar

Agriculture

Many people, both women and men, are farmers of one kind or another. They may grow their own food, keep animals, or work on large farms and plantations where peanuts and cotton are grown.

Food for the Family

In Senegal, men own the land, but women do almost all the work and produce the food. In the south, people work on small plots of land and grow **sorghum**, millet, rice, and maize (corn). In the north, where the dry climate makes it difficult to grow many crops, people keep animals for their milk. On special occasions, a goat may be killed, otherwise meat is rarely eaten. On the coast, many people make a living from fishing.

Peanuts

The main crops that Senegal produces to sell abroad are cotton, rice, and peanuts. However, the growing of peanuts has meant cutting down many trees in order to clear the land.

▽ When a cow is milked, only a little is taken, leaving plenty for the calf.

△ Peanut mountain. Peanuts are exported and used to make peanut oil.

Growing peanuts year after year is not good for the soil, and peanut fields use up land that could be used for growing food crops. This means that Senegal has to buy more food from other countries.

The Price of Food

Senegal grows two-thirds of the food it needs, and it buys the rest from other countries, such as rice from South-east Asia. Until recently, economic policies have meant that imported food was quite cheap, making it difficult for local farmers to compete. In 1994, however, Senegalese money became less valuable than money from other countries. This meant that things bought abroad were more expensive. As a result, people are now buying more local goods.

Drought and Locusts

In many places the dry climate makes it difficult to grow crops. It doesn't rain as much as it did 20 years ago. Regular **droughts** create enormous problems, but are not the only problem that farmers face. Sometimes crops are ruined by plagues of locusts, which can eat a farmer's entire crop overnight.

Industry

Industry in Senegal is changing. Many factory closings have left many people jobless. New industries, such as tourism and filmmaking, have not yet created enough new jobs.

Mineral Resources

As Senegal has no resources that can be used to make energy, it must import oil. In the ground in east Senegal there is iron ore, copper, gold, and marble that could bring in a lot of money for the country. Unfortunately these resources lie in very remote areas and it would cost a great deal to mine and use the minerals. Phosphates, which are used to make fertilizers, are mined near Thiès and are a major export.

△ Working on a loom to make fabric

Industry Today

When Senegal was a colony of France, many factories were set up to produce goods to sell to other countries in West Africa. These countries have now set up their own industries and no longer need to buy things from Senegal. Many factories have closed down in Senegal, and things that used to be made here, for example shoes and galvanized sheet metal, no longer are.

In the past, some of Senegal's industries were set up to process imported goods, such as refineries for processing oil. These refineries are now very old, outdated and run-down, and the government cannot afford to repair them.

Making a Living

With so much unemployment, people do whatever they can to earn money. In the markets of Dakar you will find people weaving baskets, carving wooden bowls, or even hammering together briefcases made from aluminum cans. Oxfam supports women's groups who set up small businesses to do things such as dye fabric, raise chickens, and make leather belts.

Tourism

Senegal has a well-developed tourist industry with 200,000 visitors a year, mainly from France and Germany. The country's attractions include its beautiful sandy beaches, excellent climate, and animal and bird reserves. However, much of the tourist industry's profits go to the foreign companies who own the leisure centers in Senegal.

▽ Senegal's birdlife provides much interest for tourists.

Challenges

All over the world, countries face problems and difficulties. Senegal is no exception.

Drought

Since 1970 the **Sahel** has suffered an almost continuous **drought.** Many wells and rivers have dried up, and people find it more and more difficult to grow food for themselves. Some people think that these are the effects of **global warming** and that the drop in rainfall is due to car fumes and industries in Europe.

Foreign Debt

Like many other countries, one of the biggest problems facing Senegal is the amount of money it borrows from other countries in order to develop. In order to repay the debt, the government has had to stop spending money on many things.

No new schools have been built, which means that many children cannot go to school. Those who can are in very large classes with few books. The government can no longer afford to pay people such as doctors, teachers, and agricultural advisors.

The problem of foreign debt has affected people in different ways. The fisherfolk of St. Louis are finding that their catches are much smaller than they were a few years ago.

They have little for themselves to eat and even less to sell on the market. This is because large, modern European ships are catching most of the fish. It used to be illegal for European boats to fish off the coast of Senegal, but because the government needs money, it agreed that the Europeans could pay for the right to fish here. The fisherfolk of St. Louis get none of this money.

Overcoming Poverty

Most people in Senegal are determined to improve their lives. In towns and villages they have joined together to form self-help groups. Some groups have set up clubs in which everyone puts a little money in every month. They take turns borrowing some of the money for an emergency or to help start a small business, for example. Other groups seek advice and information from experts about raising their animals.

◁ People in Senegal know that being able to read and write will give them confidence and independence.

▽ The fishing boats are called *pirogues*. They are sometimes used for racing.

Namarel

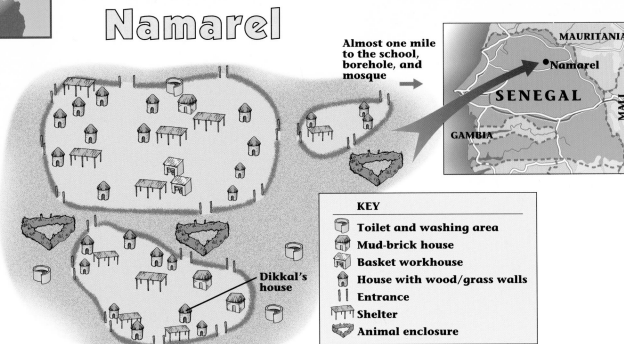

Almost one mile to the school, borehole, and mosque →

MAURITANIA

•Namarel

SENEGAL

GAMBIA

MALI

Dikkal's house

KEY

Toilet and washing area
Mud-brick house
Basket workhouse
House with wood/grass walls
Entrance
Shelter
Animal enclosure

Map of Namarel showing where Dikkal Sow lives

The village of Namarel lies in the Ferlo region of northern Senegal.

To get to Namarel from the nearest town 37 miles away, you travel on a road that is no more than a track, across a flat landscape of sandy soil and low-lying shrubs. Every now and then you see a baobab tree, often called "an upside-down tree," because it looks as though it has its roots in the air. In a landscape like this, where everything looks the same, it would be very difficult for you to find the village, but Mustapha Dia, who comes from this area, says, "When you've lived here all your life, you can navigate by the sun and by using signs—trees and the way the land looks."

The Climate in Namarel

The Ferlo region is part of the **Sahel.** The wet season lasts from July to October, but rain is unreliable and quickly soaked up by the dry, sandy soil. The **harmattan** wind blows from the Sahara desert,causing sandstorms so fierce, sometimes you cannot see your hand in front of your face. Between March and July, the hot season, daytime temperatures can be as high as 113° F.

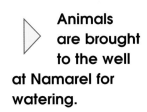

Animals are brought to the well at Namarel for watering.

Many people living in Namarel can remember a time when the rainfall was much higher and many different types of plants grew. In the last 20 years however, the climate has changed, and there is now much less rain.

Dikkal with her older brother and his baby.

Dikkal Sow

Dikkal Sow loves living in Namarel. She loves the landscape, and she loves her family and her many friends. People in Namarel always look after each other.

Dikkal Sow is eight, the youngest in her family. She has two brothers and two sisters. Her parents own some **irrigated** millet fields near the Sénégal River, 37 miles away, and they are often away looking after the crops. Dikkal has plenty of aunts and uncles to look after her.

Village Life

The People

The people who live in Namarel belong to the Peulh group. They are **seminomadic pastoralists.** During the dry season, some of them move around the region with their animals, mainly cows and goats, in search of water and food. Sometimes their wicker huts can be seen near the Sénégal River during the dry season. During the wet season they return to their villages. The money from selling their animals is the herder's main income.

Many young people leave Namarel to look for work in Dakar, or even as far away as Paris, France. But people always keep in touch with their village, and, if they can, they return to help. A group of people from Namarel who were studying in Dakar set up an organization called ADENA, which runs many activities, such as health, agriculture, and literacy training in the area.

Water is collected from deep wells.

△ Ousseynou Wally, the local carpenter, makes a bed from branches lashed together.

The Village Place

Dikkal's village is made up of three large compounds, where members of her **extended family** live. The houses are made out of natural materials—mud bricks, wood, and woven grass. These houses are cooler than the concrete buildings in the village, such as the school, the dispensary (where medicines are given out), and the millet store.

Namarel has four small shops that sell rice and dried fish. But these things are expensive, as they have to be brought from far away. If people want anything else, such as clothing, they have to travel a long way to one of the towns. Apart from these necessities, people are more or less **self-sufficient.**

People in Namarel cannot take water for granted like we do. They don't get it from a faucet but from pumps in deep boreholes that have to be drilled. People in Namarel pay for the water they use, and this money is used to keep the pump in good repair.

School

The school in Namarel is one of the few concrete buildings in the village. Dikkal has been going to school for four months, but she says she hasn't really gotten used to it yet! Because the government can only afford one teacher for the school, only-one third of the children can go at any one time. And only children who live in Namarel or near enough to walk can go, as there is no transportation to and from the school. In the classroom there are very few books and pens.

School Subjects

There are 44 pupils in Dikkal's class. Most are the same age as her, but there are also some 14-year-olds who are learning different things. They are studying for their Elementary School Certificate and entrance exam for secondary, or high school. They study French, mathematics, the history and geography of Senegal and Africa, drawing, and singing. To take the exam, pupils must go to N'Dioum, 37 miles away. Some may be unable to pay for the transportation there.

▽ **Dikkal's classroom**

△ **Dikkal's group learns reading, writing, mathematics, singing, and sports.**

Alassane Diouf, the teacher, teaches the children things that will be useful to them in their home lives, such as how to grow vegetables, how to build stoves that don't burn too much wood, and how to help their parents. He sometimes buys pens and books out of his own salary for the children to use.

Language

Although Dikkal speaks Pulaar at home with her family, at school she is taught in French. As she doesn't understand French, the teacher has to help her a lot. Many adults are now going to classes to learn to read and write in their own language of Pulaar, as they were never taught this when they went to school. Being able to read and write is very important, as it means they won't have to ask others to read things for them. It gives them more independence. Only recently, books in the Pulaar language began to be produced, and they are very popular.

Spare Time

Dikkal does lots of jobs to help her family, and sometimes there isn't a lot of time left for playing games. Luckily, Dikkal enjoys many of her chores.

Playing Games

When she does have some spare time, Dikkal likes playing a game called *tenge.* She throws a stone in the air and has to pick up other stones, which lay on the ground, in ones or twos before it lands. It's very similar to a game called jacks. Dikkal has lots of friends, and they like playing with dolls together. They pretend the dolls are real children, and they make the dolls fetch water and wood just like they do.

Festivals

Ramadan is a very special month of the year when Muslims **fast.** Dikkal is too young to fast, but she will fast when she is 15. People who are fasting go without food and drink from sunrise until sunset.

Juulde Korka is a festival that takes place at the end of Ramadan. It is known as Eid-ul-Fitr by Muslims in other countries. Each family celebrates by eating, singing, and dancing. Dikkal enjoys the celebrations very much, because she says, "everyone is happy."

Dikkal plays tenge in the doorway of her home.

The Cultural Group

There are no phones in Namarel. There isn't even a local radio station, but residents are hoping to start one soon. Even without these modern conveniences, it is not difficult to find out about local news. A group of musicians travels from village to village singing songs about the past, the Peulh culture, and things that have happened in other villages, such as a baby being born. They also sing songs about environmental issues to help people to care for the land. Their shows include singing and drumming, and they are very popular. Mbourel Dia, the main singer, is a **grio.**

Visitors in the village are always offered food, drink, and somewhere to stay. People eat together from one large dish. The villagers make sure the guest gets the best bits of food. After the meal, the traditional three cups of strong sweet mint tea are brewed and then poured into small cups from a height so that they are frothy.

▽ Dikkal enjoys learning songs about the Peulh people and their history from the cultural group.

A Day with Dikkal

Getting up and Going to School

Dikkal is woken up by her aunt before sunrise. This is the coolest part of the day, and people get up early to get their jobs done before it is too hot. Outside the compound is a fenced-off area where Dikkal washes, using a cup to pour water over herself from a bucket.

Dikkal walks to school with her friends and gets there by 8 a.m. At midmorning, pupils have their breakfast. They eat so late because they have to wait for the cattle to be brought in and milked.

Afternoon Chores

School finishes at 1 P.M., and Dikkal goes home to eat lunch and do chores. She prefers working at home to going to school. Dikkal goes out with her friends to fetch wood from a tree called *kelli*, which burns slowly.

▽ **Fary Diallo works at the market garden.**

Dikkal helps feed the calves and collects water from the faucet just about a mile away. Water is piped to the faucet from the well in Namarel. Dikkal's family is lucky to be near a water source—some people have to walk a long way every day to get water. Sometimes she helps one of her older sisters tend their mother's vegetable patch, where they grow onions and cabbages. Two afternoons a week she has to go back to school for another two hours.

When boys are not at school, their job is to look after the animals. Even boys as young as six are responsible for a small herd. They leave with the herd early in the morning and spend the day with the animals looking for food.

Evening Relaxation

The evening meal, which Dikkal helps her aunt cook, is usually *lacciri*. This is a kind of **couscous** made from millet served with milk. Sometimes they have lamb, goat, or chicken with the couscous. It is dark by 7 P.M., and there is no electricity. The family sits by the fire talking about the day or telling stories, or they go to visit friends and elderly people. Caring about the elderly is very important in Senegal.

△ Dikkal helps her aunt pound the millet for the evening meal.

In Namarel no one has a car, and people get around by walking. Most things that need to be transported around the village are carried. However, people have come up with clever ideas to move heavier things.

Transporting Water

Water is needed for cooking, washing, and drinking and also for the animals. In this hot climate everyone needs a lot of water. To collect water, people fill inner tubes from tractor tires at the well. These are loaded onto the backs of donkeys or carts.

Traveling out of the Village

Roads into Namarel are nothing more than rough tracks in the sand. Vehicles don't often come along, but when a truck does visit the village it is packed with people taking advantage of the opportunity to visit. If you see another vehicle driving in this area, you always stop to chat and find out the latest news.

If people need to go to the hospital or to buy or sell things, they have to go to N'Dioum, 37 miles away. They usually have to walk, and this takes more than a day. If they're lucky, they might get a lift in a passing vehicle. People cannot use bicycles, because the wheels would get stuck in the sand.

A cart hurries off with its load of water.

Filling inner tubes with water at the borehole

The Costs of Transportation

Transportation is a big problem for people in Namarel. Transportation costs push up the price of anything that comes from the towns, making these things very expensive. Everyone in Namarel hopes that ADENA will soon be able to buy a vehicle that people could use to transport animals to the town to sell and to carry goods back. It could also be used as an ambulance.

Journeys around Senegal

If you were to visit Senegal, you would probably fly into Yof, the international airport. From here it is a short taxi or bus ride into Dakar, the capital city, just eight miles away.

Getting around Dakar

For those who can afford taxi fares, getting around Dakar is quite easy. For most people in Senegal, however, even bus fares are too expensive, and they must walk. There are no sidewalks or crossings and, unfortunately, there are many accidents involving pedestrians. Even more accidents are caused because many buses are old, in a bad shape, and unsafe.

Buses

Buses travel from Dakar to and between all the major towns. People on the buses visit friends in other towns, go to Dakar to look for work, or return to their villages to help out on the land.

▽ You often see buses with luggage piled high on their roofs on the main roads.

The Ferry

Le Joola ferry sails twice a week in each direction between Dakar and Basse Casamance. The journey takes 17 hours, but it is a lot easier than traveling over land. The ferry is an important route for traders taking goods to and from Senegal's capital. It sometimes seems more like a floating market than a boat with its cargo of fruit and vegetables, live chickens, dried fish, and spices from Casamance and manufactured **consumer goods** from the city.

Trains

From the old station right in the center of Dakar you can get a train to Bamako in Mali, or to the town of St. Louis in the north. Thiès is an important train junction, and work on the railroads provides important employment for the people of the town.

▷ Taxis lined up outside the station in Dakar.

Poeple who can afford it can fly on one of *Air Senegal's* flights to St. Louis, Ziguinchor, and Tambacounda. Most towns have a small runway, but few people can afford to travel by air. They take the bus, the train, or the ferry instead.

Images of Senegal

Women work together to support each other and improve their lives.

This man is picking pods to feed his goats.

In a short book like this is it very difficult to tell you everything there is to know about Senegal. It is a country full of many contrasts— of desert and forest, wealth and poverty, city and village.

You have read of some of the difficulties facing many Senegalese people. People would be quick to tell you, however, how they face up to these challenges with strength and determination.

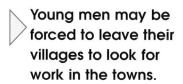 Young men may be forced to leave their villages to look for work in the towns.

▽ Many women borrow money from their groups to start a small business, such as this market stall.

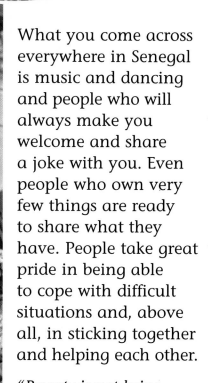

What you come across everywhere in Senegal is music and dancing and people who will always make you welcome and share a joke with you. Even people who own very few things are ready to share what they have. People take great pride in being able to cope with difficult situations and, above all, in sticking together and helping each other.

"Poverty is not being without clothes: the person who is truly poor is the one who has nobody."
—Wolof proverb

Glossary

Colony A country taken over by another Country.

Consumer goods Things manufactured in factories that people buy for their homes, such as TVs, radios, and washing machines.

Couscous A dish of steamed, crushed wheat.

Drought A long period of time with no, or very little, rain.

Enclave A country completely surrounded by another.

Exports Goods that are sold to other countries.

Extended family In Western society, the nuclear family is more common and includes just parents and children. An extended family includes grandparents, aunts, uncles, cousins, and even more distant relatives.

Fast To go without food for a period of time, often for religious reasons.

Global warming The effect of increasing the earth's temperature caused by pollution and industrialization.

Griots The people in the community who tell the stories, sometimes by singing.

Harmattan A hot wind that blows from the Sahara desert.

Human rights The things that all human beings are entitled to, including the right to be able to say what one wants and not to be discriminated against because of religious or political beliefs.

Irrigation A system of providing water for plants by means of pipes and channels.

Mangrove A group of low trees with exposed roots, usually found in tropical swamps.

Monsoon Seasonal wind that often brings rain.

Multiparty democracy A political system in which anyone can set up a political party and ask for people to vote for him or her.

Muslims People who follow the Islamic religion.

Nomadic A lifestyle followed by people who travel around, usually with animals, looking for pasture.

Oral tradition The tradition of passing on a community's history from generation to generation by telling stories.

Pastoralists People who make a living from herding animals and selling their products, such as their skins, meat, and milk.

Peninsula A piece of land surrounded on three sides by water.

Sahel An Arabic word meaning "on the edge." It is the area on the edge of the Sahara.

Self-sufficient When people are able to grow enough food to feed themselves and their families and produce all the other things that they need without relying on other people.

Seminomadic People who travel around for the dry part of the year looking for pasture.

Sorghum A tropical grain.

Tropical The part of the world between the tropics of Cancer and Capricorn.

Index

About Oxfam

Oxfam America works in partnership with communities in Asia, Africa, the Americas, and the Caribbean to find long-term solutions to poverty and hunger. Oxfam America supports the self-help efforts of poor people—especially women, landless farm workers, and survivors of war and natural disasters—who are working to make their lives better. Oxfam America believes that all people have the basic rights to earn a living and to have food, shelter, health care, and education.

Oxfam America is part of the international family of Oxfam organizations that work in more than 80 countries, including Senegal, where Oxfam's established program concentrates on the country's poorest regions. Oxfam supports landless people, both rural and urban, by providing training, legal advice, and agricultural technology. Oxfam also helps people to claim their basic rights through work with community and women's groups and with trade unions, aiming to strengthen these organizations through leadership training. Many of Senegal's largest development organizations started with funding from Oxfam. Oxfam is also helping poor people in Senegal to improve their living conditions by working with local groups to train health educators and literacy workers.

This edition © 1997 Rigby Education
Published by Rigby Interactive Library,
an imprint of Rigby Education,
division of Reed Elsevier, Inc.
500 Coventry Lane
Crystal Lake, IL 60014

Printed in Great Britain by Bath Press Colourbooks, Glasgow
Designed and produced by Visual Image
Cover design by Threefold Design

00 99 98 97 96
10 9 8 7 6 5 4 3 2 1

Library of Congress Cataloging-in-Publication Data

Brownlie, Alison, 1949–
    Senegal / Alison Brownlie.
       p.   cm. -- (Worldfocus)
    Includes index.
    Summary: Introduces the geography, history, culture, and economics of the West African country of Senegal and provides a close-up look at the life a young girl living in the village of Namarel.
    ISBN 1-57572-076-0
    1. Senegal--Juvenile literature. [1. Senegal.] I. Title. II. Series.
DT549.22.B76   1996
966.3--dc20   95-26778

Acknowledgments

The publisher would like to thank the following for their help in preparing this book: David Waller of Oxfam's West Africa Desk; Bob Gibson and François Diop and staff of Oxfam's Senegal office; Jenny Lunnon, who gathered the information about Namarel, and James Hawkins for the photographs; Ousemane Pam, Dikel Gadjiga, Fatou Oumar Seck, Mustapha Dia, Moussa Sow, Abdoulaye Gallo Bâ, Alassane Diouf, Dikkal Sow, and all the people of ADENA (l'Assocation pour le Développement de Namarel); Aminata Abdoulaye Seck of Project Integré de Podor; Tracey Hawkins of Oxfam's photo library; and Angela Grunsell, Oxfam Primary Education Advisor, who commented on early drafts.

The author and publisher also wish to acknowledge, with thanks, the following photographic sources:
Cover photograph: Oxfam; D. Brown/Oxfam: p. 12; Alison Brownlie, pp. 4, 6, 25; Jeremy Hartley/Oxfam, pp. 5, 7, 8, 12c, 15, 24, 26, 28t, 29; James Hawkins, pp. 10, 11, 15b, 16–23, 28b.